The Picture Never Taken

Sam Gardiner

Smith/Doorstop Books

Published 2004 by
Smith/Doorstop Books
The Poetry Business
The Studio
Byram Arcade
Westgate
Huddersfield HD1 1ND

Copyright © Sam Gardiner 2004
All Rights Reserved

ISBN 1-902382-66-8

Typeset at The Poetry Business
Printed by Peepal Tree Press, Leeds
The Poetry Business gratefully acknowledges the help of
Kirklees Metropolitan Council and Arts Council England.

Acknowledgements
Some of these poems have appeared previously in the
following publications: *Areté, Poetry London, The Rialto,
TLS*.

Sam Gardiner received an Arts Council Writers' Award
in 2002.

CONTENTS

5	The Picture Never Taken
6	To Breathe Were Life
8	Dedicated
9	All Things Are Becoming
10	The Calling
11	Dear You
12	No Surprise
13	Second Person
14	Creased
15	Orithea
16	Bridge
17	Believe it
18	Strokkur Saga
20	Python
22	Short Circuitry
24	Smile
26	Variations
27	Chairs
28	Pale Reds
29	Kingfisher
30	The Wreath

THE PICTURE NEVER TAKEN

Who knows what storms brought him here,
Shaking the shine from his overcoat,
Hanging it on the hallstand by the throat
And combing the rain-clouds from his hair.

No need to ransack the archives to recall
Him barging scrubbed from the scullery,
The picture never taken goes before me,
His face patched with scraps of Lurgan Mail

Middled with red, which fluttered across
The fields as the day wore on, went from him
In small dismissals, cuts won yet lost.
Stubbled with shadow, war-worn from the fight,
His coming home was straight into the east room,
Where darkness gathered, to say good night.

TO BREATHE WERE LIFE

No 'as though' about it, Ulysses

Loaded with smouldering crates
Of beech leaves, barges work the canals
In an aromatic mist, past cottages

Ankle deep in pollen, among trees which can
Dance and rain privately, long
After the rain has gone.

Ears level with the ripe barley,
An Indian brave searches Ruddle's Acre
For a lost inhaler.

By his deathbed, beside Dr Potter's
Asthma Remedy, lies the sixgun he shot
His cousin with. Boys get lots

Of practice dying, clawing at
Doses of lead, lurching, falling flat.
But not this weightless hanging about

High against the ceiling, looking down
At his discarded body, nor the tombstone
Talk of his parents as they warm

Their hands at the best bedroom fire,
And fight quietly over whether
Mum's 'God took his breath away' is better

Than his father's 'Killed in action'.
Alive again, 'for ever panting and forever young',
Ever older but panting still, to string

Beans as his mother's white breath rises grey
On the sunlit wall; alive to envy
His father pushing him up Lisnisky

Lane on the bar of his bike, breathing as if
For both of them, satisfied that there is
Only one universe, and this is it.

DEDICATED

to the old house where a shrub
hugs the chimney and yellow flowers nod
along the eaves; to those who ordered
Edgar Allan from my chamber, who shook
the woodlice from my socks and taught
my legs to walk to the shop
for cigarette cards; to rivers, trees and
constellations so smart they look careless; to
high fields grazed by clouds, invisible sheep
with mulberry shadows, and that lake among
the hills lying in its own light;
to Sunday League supporters, including a maple
from whose packed grandstand a thousand flags
wave in the home team's colours; to
the pleasure horse that goes clap trap
claptrap down the lane, where the wind
swings on an infirm fence and both
fall over, one runs off across the
fields, the other just lies there; to
Harvest Acres with its fast and slow
food joints and stores with cupolas on
which weathercocks gyrate and crow in unison;
to those commanded to 'Keep your cabins,
you scum, you do assist the storm'
who come buffeting about the deck speaking
in tongues, instead of without, as is
more conventional with us; to the inexpressible,
bless them, they shall be expressed (and
to Eileen for fetching me a pound
of hyphens jangling in a plastic bag
(needlessly, as it happens)); without whom and
which this might not have been written.

ALL THINGS ARE BECOMING

i.e. coming to pass without the passing

Falling is an uprush of surroundings,
overhead fields, heaving floors
and delicate insidious roots
fingering the foundations.

This end of the room, now given over
to a dead leaf dance, was once a grove
of wooden legs, a table and four bony chairs
each with four, though sometimes the chairs
had six and clumped about.

                         But whatever
the generations underfoot stood for,
lied for around that vanished table,
went weaving off in eight-legged coffins
to the gate where time has no passage.

The house is home to absences. Rafters
fend off skies of slate, while in the walls
bricks once densely mortared
now balance beyond falling.

THE CALLING

'Sam,' she called, a voice from the crowd,
urgent, excited. I turned and smiled
in vague apology – Should we know each other?
May we? – in the direction of a knot
of young women unravelling in
all directions. One, cold and pink
wearing a zigzagged jacket, was looking at
or past me. 'Sam,' she repeated, more loudly,
the callee being slow of hearing, 'Sam!',
and a pre-playschool toddler trotted up and
took her hand. I walked on, taking a long-cut,
saved the embarrassment of being somewhere
even earlier. Sorry, Sam's mum, but thanks
for calling. I can't remember the last time
anyone summoned me like that. Yes, I can:
my young mother, from the lighted doorway.

DEAR YOU

Delighted to have daylight to see you by
as night to not, to watch you taking shape
from inside out in labial pink and cherry,
composing your risen self in silksoft lamina,
blue on blue, leaf smoke on sky. And then,

dear you, making leary mouths in the glass
and spending ages on the face that ages
before you. Had I been myself I could have
told you you weren't yours, in that lipstickless
self-portrait in reverse, the mirror's invention.

I can write it now you're gone, have left me
my self again (I tell myself), alone with words
in a room. Poetry is for those who need it,
you say, who don't, defining the heart's need,
provoking love notes you will never read.

NO SURPRISE

No surprise to come down
to an armful of presents
gift-wrapped to deceive,
by an expert at creative tension

between content and form,
who is also and unavoidably
a sporadic donor of
ironic templates for dull cheeses.

No surprise that perched on each
is a spider of string,
nor that the rolled calendar
glugs and the book rattles.

SECOND PERSON

You rush into the shopping arcade
and step aside to avoid the mirror-clad pillar
when you meet yourself rushing out.

Swiftly you pass, and may even glance
over your shoulder just in time to glimpse
yourself spinning on your heel,

wondering which of you is real. As I did,
before hurrying off, getting home first
and trying to persuade her there was only one

of me. But apparently she had always known
there were two, and the one she loved
should soon be home, if I'd care to wait.

CREASED

She must have seen it coming,
she who invented second sight,
when my ruby-eyed family group
appeared very slightly creased,
but not altogether beyond mention.
Creases is rich, she said, coming,
she said, from you who can't tell
a surf- from an ironing-board.
Thus the terrible trivialities
accumulate around the potbound
begonias,
        until tonight:
                a shot sang out,
a thing shot out, a shout went up,
she fell, and all her hollows rang.
Why else would I be reading
'Porphyria's Lover' over and over.
Why else would I have come
into the darkened kitchen,
placed two empty beakers
on the mercury draining-board,
and now be angling them
until they fill with moonlight.

ORITHEA

Not a wind, not a breath, more an effect
without a cause trembled the curtain,
pure movement only, a breeze inhaling.
Until, realizing where it was,

it swept your still unopened letter

to the floor, and slammed the door
as it left. Last spring, April, actually
the sixteenth, Boreas the north wind
carried Orithea off to the mountains,

where she bore him many little breezes.

They grow into winds, gales, storms,
and are streaming this way, slinging slates
at conservatories, mugging trees
and pushing the clouds around.

The postmark is illegible, mysterious,

as postmarks should be, but no one else
makes ees like that. Or would have leapt up,
flung the door aside and joined
the hailstorm dancing on the lawn.

BRIDGE

During your absence someone has built
a bridge between us, soaring above the river
you splashed across by ferry,
a blue suspension of girders, bars and cables
in pressure and tension, straining
one against the other for that great co-operative
leap from bank to bank.

If you came back you would ride the bridge,
and be white-eyed by Heraclitus
the Scamander-stepper, a warning that to begin
again you would have to go back too far,
back to before you knew it was a mistake
but couldn't keep your hands to yourself.

But we were never much good with bridges,
spent our lives going the long way round
on narrow B roads beneath broad skies,
past places where one more wrong turning
might have seen us right.

BELIEVE IT

You won't believe it when it happens,
you who believe in everything but God
(or in nothing but), may not even
know it has happened, though you felt
lighter inside than out, floated above yourself,
flinched at the cold breath of passing
wings, and almost embarked on a ship
made out of fog, the night sailing.

Look at you now, like a blind
ass in an olive mill being led
by another's tail, xylophoning your prison bars,
conjuring up small blue icebergs peppered with
grit in an eau-de-Nil lagoon.
Heatwaves and ice years prolong the detention
(how they quarry the cliffs into truck-sized
blocks that need shifting), as does your
garden of labelled sticks and being desensitised
by the sweet Grecian smell of creosote.

Trees are simply green things without thoughts
that stand in our way. Only by
becoming brainless ourselves can we
                              understand them.
Same goes for olives, quasars, genes, love,
you name it. Don't you wish that
worry wasn't the highest form of imagination?
What matters is that nothing matters, except
that you keep your instruments keen, in
working order, ticking over and alert, ready
for when it happens. And it will.

STROKKUR SAGA

Again they assemble round the pond,
Audur Soft-Voice, Melkorka the Beautiful,
Louis Camel-Lip and Wystan the Rugose,
Olaf the Peacock, Gunnlaug Snake-Tongue,
to admire a symbol of nothing but itself,
the monumental irreverence of physics,
the delinquent gesture. As they came,
we have come. We wait. Stillness grows.

The all-night sun unrolls the hinterland.
Clouds pass on airbeds. At last a bubble
as big as a greenhouse floats up, pulsates
beneath the surface, and bursts skywards
in a spout higher than a plumber's nightmare.
With a ripple of invisible muscles the wind
wrestles the plume of water and bends
an exclamation mark to a question.

A wet translucence descends to the east,
On Ketil Flat-Nose with his camcorder
whose Inuit blood draws him to leeward.
Strokkur the Joker falls flat and, once bolt-
holed, grins up from its sulphurous puddle.
As we plod off, baby geysers gurgle
and plop, their round mouths encrusted
with the pastel yolk of boiled rocks.

Once you have seen it once you can get on
with the rest of your life, with this dish
of scrambled egg, windows of winter sunshine
and a lacuna in thought where Strokkur,
sunless and snowbound, still circles the Pole,

unceasing and unseen and pumping darkness
for itself and for the mechanistic stars,
who flicker with vertiginous applause.

PYTHON

Five minutes before time began,
and there was nothing much to say
except *Don't*, God promised Her
daughter an Earth for a playball.
Now meet the Man behind God,
and the Python behind the Man
behind God, who spoiled the sport.

Poor serpent, sun-shafted by
Apollo, de-shanked by Jehovah,
never had much luck with gods.
Born to symbolise more than most,
Python does so curled up beneath
a good newspaper in your
local pet shop in Parnassus Avenue.

Never intending to be seen, nor
meant to be, nor named, he failed
on all fronts and is called Patrick,
this fearsome weekend hunter who rolls
himself like a hosepipe round a dream
of asphyxiation, of stifling his supper
in dark rain at blood temperature.

Enter a slack-mouthed waiter bearing
a tray of dead rats, humming
the all-time hit, *Being you is easier
than being me*. His gravy-brown
hair hangs inert when, quick
as a lizard, he abstracts the licked spoon
and dishes up a farm-fresh rodent.

Five minutes before time ends, when
there is nothing left to say except
I told you so, Python dozes open-eyed
beneath an oracular broadsheet,
waiting anxiously for the next god
to come along looking for some-
one to blame when it all goes wrong.

SHORT CIRCUITRY

> *'Everything is what it is
> and not another thing'* – Bishop Butler

A mutant is being questioned about the
Retirement Park murders. Last night a 40-
seater coach was found abandoned in Weelsby
Woods, where autumn has torched the trees.
One bald bearded couple left a note:
the sun caught fire and sank; please
send replacement. And transparencies of black images
with white shadows, soon to be ghosts.

Bargain basements are carnivals on Giro days.
A toddler in a green mac pedals
a new red tractor by the Freshney,
past three headless swans. Storm damaged fences
are being reclaimed, the storm having blown
itself away. A claw hammer pulls nails
screeching from the timber. This has no
bearing on that, nor that on this.

All is in a mind, joined by
thought as if there were meanings outside,
so listen to what the experts say
and you will hear the exact opposite
as well, then it is up or
down to you to make your mind.
But let's enquire further and when no
one answers let's go round the back.

There may be someone in the garden
digging a dugout, pit, sump, or something,
the spade helping itself to wormy portions

of earthcake, and a green woodpecker clinging
to the brick cliff like an alpinist,
or mortarpecker, this not being one of
those tales which for want of ??
and !! lead somewhere, but nowhere else.

SMILE

From the makers of expressions for photographs
and suppliers to schools and hospices worldwide,
a selection of our most collectable smiles:
the kid's through long sobbed-for ice cream;
       the smiles given by those with little else;
the smiles of passengers grounded by fog
who crack every gag in the Nervous
Flyer's Joke Book; the smile of landing lights;
       the once seen lady's, sweet and kind,
smiling and spinning at her wheel, you
did but see her driving by and
yet you love her till you die;
       the smile that couldn't keep its lips
to itself, and later can't remember any
of that, just her brass bedhead's polished
globes in which his faces were reflected;
       the smiles we gave the tree that
groweth in the midst of the garden,
having hung back on its branches the
fruit of the knowledge of false opposites;
       the smile when she says 'Cut out
the bloody levity' and leaves behind only
her scent, sweet and sour, his favourite;
the smiles more beautiful on plainer faces;
       the hermit's on returning to his maisonette
bearing pepper, no more than a bee
can carry, in a twist of scripture,
knowing that only God and he exist;
       the smile that, having noticed how each
raindrop inverts the garden, a galaxy of
small worlds upside down against the glass,
goes out to investigate and returns inscrutable;

        the immortal's when he announces in Homebase
that he is nearly 88 and needs
a lawnmower with a five-year warranty, minimum;
the smiles of the Early Church, so-called
        because of its exceptionally early rising and
other forms of asceticism, whose funerals went
dancing through the streets waving psalm trees
and singing 'The dead are never sad';
        smiles that trivialise terrors, ensconcing us into
seeming knowledge when we should submit ourselves
to an unknown fear; and the face
of desolation which can still, somehow, smile.

VARIATIONS

on a sentence by Tolstoy

The bishop came on deck and as he
was pacing up and down he noticed a
group of men near the prow listening to
a fisherman who was pointing at the sea.

The pointing man beside the prow as it
was pacing the sea listened to a bishop
near where the deck was coming up and
down as the group of fishermen had noticed.

A fisherman came on the bishop who was
on deck listening to a group of men
near the prow who had noticed the sea
and were pointing and pacing up and down.

The grouped men were pacing up and down
and as they neared the prow a fisherman
who had been listening noticed that the bishop
was pointing at the sea coming on deck.

The fishermen came on deck and as they
were listening to the man near the pointing
prow they noticed a group of bishops who
were pacing up and down on the sea.

CHAIRS

The chair I chose of the four,
the one left warm when no longer
occupied with her wordless sitting and being
what she was before she gathered up
her keys, turned and batted both eyelids
at the nicotine ceilinged café, and became
a faint footprint on a wet street,

was once a beechnut, one of four
in a pig-haired silk-lined purse
mislaid beneath a hedge by a dormouse
ready for bed one mist-hung night
when there were owls and lovers about,

and became a tree, a gesture against
the vast emptiness, which dripped herbicide to
keep the weeds from scuffling around its
overground roots, great hammer-toed feet the
ploughboy's girl who came to bring him
a bloater sandwich stumbled over into an
embrace the wind in the branches sang
and waved the pinkish female and purplish
male flowers about about, but when October
took the wood by storm, the tree

became a party of beech chairs, scraping
their feet, cooling down and climbing onto
the tables, because of which and of
being the only one left I left.

PALE REDS

Some white-collared body
in the rectory garden
is dead-heading fused roses.

By the sunlit door a three-
or four-year old, immovable
beneath a pink umbrella,

is praying for rain.
Deep indoors a solo cello
bumbles and belly laughs

and a warplane rips open
those pale red roofs,
this chestnut cobbled path.

KINGFISHER

There never was a rich uncle who sent you
postal orders; there was a bow-fronted
Mrs Twinem who paid you buttons for your
sharp eyes, needles and sleepless fingers.

There was a pseudo-Regency sideboard
saved from the big house, dark wood
that swigged beeswax and glowed
with appreciation, the imposter.

There never was a stream at the garden end,
only a shallow ditch where water
never coursed, and a kingfisher
no one but you believed in.

In the residents' courtyard two bronzed gardeners,
radio among the shrubs, plant new flowers
within a radius of song, weed out the old
and toss them on the shrieking barrow.

THE WREATH

The wreath I left to wither to glory
on my mother's grave, two
or three Sundays ago, had gone.
Grave to grave enquiries

traced it to one Audrey Bee,
died 1994 aged 49, much missed
by her loving husband, N F Bee,
MBE, BSc (Hons), ARICS.

No evidence exonerated Mrs Bee
from stealing my mother's wreath
by the dark of the moon, to amaze
her white-flowered nettles.

In winter the cemetery shuts itself
at six. Everyone knows this goes on.
As one of tomorrow's dead
you have today been warned.

Perhaps nobody sent her flowers,
anniversary cards, or wrote her poems
so she wrote them herself.
Still, it must be a comfort

having so many realists around
when this unreality ends, lying there
until the lights come on,
night after night.

Keep an eye on those stars for me,
Audrey, try joining up the dots:
draw me a Prince of Diamonds.
And please keep the wreath.